WOMEN DON'T POOP

& OTHER LIES

Toilet Trivia, Gender Rolls,
and the Sexist History of Pooping

Written by Bonnie Miller
Illustrated by Nicole Narváez

 ULYSSES PRESS

Published in the US by:
ULYSSES PRESS
PO Box 3440
Berkeley, CA 94703
www.ulyssespress.com

ISBN: 978-1-64604-078-0

Printed in the United States by Versa Press
10 9 8 7 6 5 4 3 2

Acquisitions editor: Casie Vogel
Project editor: Bridget Thoreson
Managing editor: Claire Chun
Editor: Anne Healey
Proofreader: Renee Rutledge
Front cover design: Nicole Narváez

This book is dedicated to the #BlackLivesMatter movement.
Go to blacklivesmatter.com to donate directly
to their profoundly important efforts.

—Bonnie & Nicole

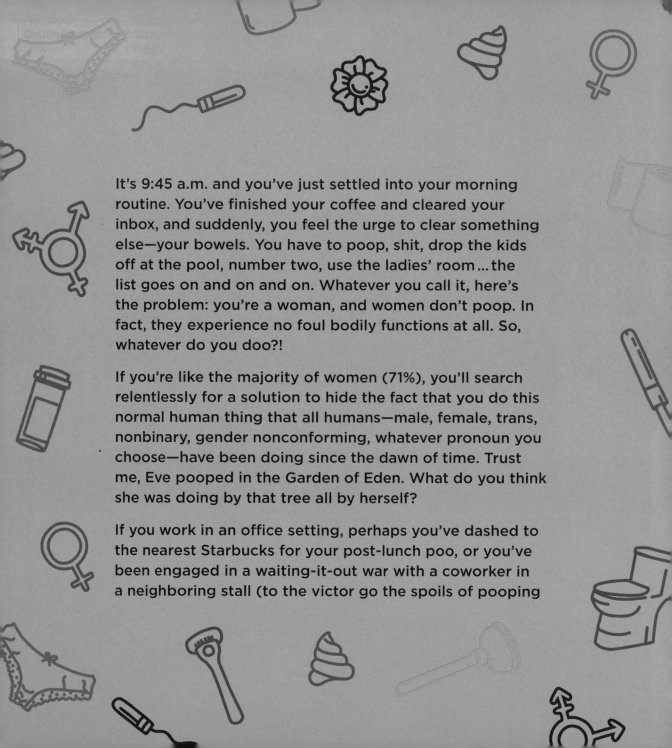

It's 9:45 a.m. and you've just settled into your morning routine. You've finished your coffee and cleared your inbox, and suddenly, you feel the urge to clear something else—your bowels. You have to poop, shit, drop the kids off at the pool, number two, use the ladies' room...the list goes on and on and on. Whatever you call it, here's the problem: you're a woman, and women don't poop. In fact, they experience no foul bodily functions at all. So, whatever do you doo?!

If you're like the majority of women (71%), you'll search relentlessly for a solution to hide the fact that you do this normal human thing that all humans—male, female, trans, nonbinary, gender nonconforming, whatever pronoun you choose—have been doing since the dawn of time. Trust me, Eve pooped in the Garden of Eden. What do you think she was doing by that tree all by herself?

If you work in an office setting, perhaps you've dashed to the nearest Starbucks for your post-lunch poo, or you've been engaged in a waiting-it-out war with a coworker in a neighboring stall (to the victor go the spoils of pooping

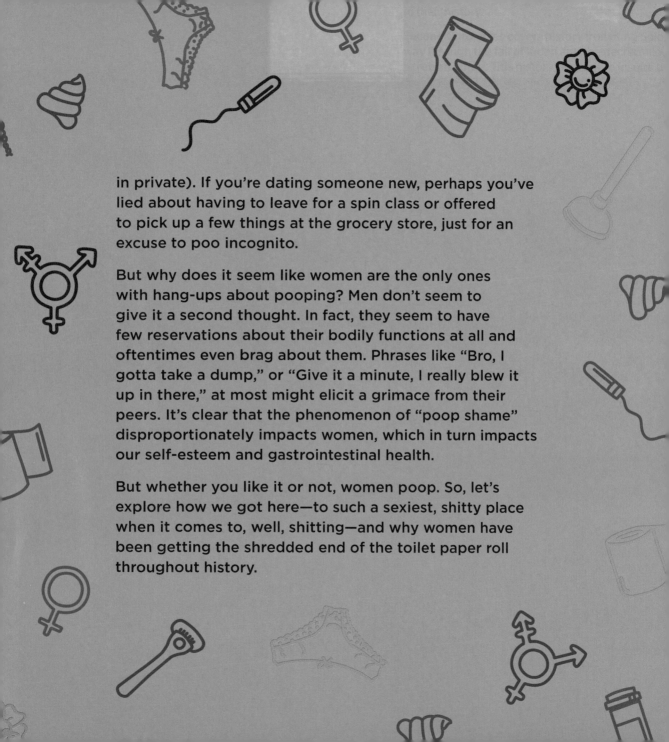

in private). If you're dating someone new, perhaps you've lied about having to leave for a spin class or offered to pick up a few things at the grocery store, just for an excuse to poo incognito.

But why does it seem like women are the only ones with hang-ups about pooping? Men don't seem to give it a second thought. In fact, they seem to have few reservations about their bodily functions at all and oftentimes even brag about them. Phrases like "Bro, I gotta take a dump," or "Give it a minute, I really blew it up in there," at most might elicit a grimace from their peers. It's clear that the phenomenon of "poop shame" disproportionately impacts women, which in turn impacts our self-esteem and gastrointestinal health.

But whether you like it or not, women poop. So, let's explore how we got here—to such a sexiest, shitty place when it comes to, well, shitting—and why women have been getting the shredded end of the toilet paper roll throughout history.

FIRST THINGS FIRST:
IF YOU'RE READING THIS,
YOU'RE A HUMAN, AND YOU POOP.

Just so we're all on the same page here—and we should be, because this is a book, after all—everybody poops. Everybody, everywhere, since forever. If you have a body, no matter the shape, size, color, or genitalia, you poop, simple as that. In fact, the average human poops 410 pounds per year and spends about 9,000 hours (one full year) on the toilet in a lifetime, at minimum. So, if you were ever under the illusion that any subset of people don't poop, I'm sorry to disappoint you. Behind closed bathroom doors, we're all the same—or at least we should be.

NEVER-
THE-
LESS...

WE POOP!

Pooping can be more difficult for women because we tend to have some different internal organs from men. And not just any organs—the ones that allow us to make new humans inside our bodies. I'm talking uteri, ovaries, fallopian tubes, the whole reproductive shebang. To accommodate these organs—and the babies that camp out in one of them for nine months—our pelvises are wider, making our colons longer than men's by about 10 centimeters (4-ish inches) on average. This means food takes longer to pass through our bodies, making us more prone to bloating and irregularity. Neat.

WHEN THEY GO LOW, WE GO—

ACTUALLY, WE SHOULD GO LOW, TOO.

Like a lot of things, modern toilets are generally built to accommodate a man's height. This leaves many women sitting either at a 90-degree angle or with their feet dangling, which just isn't ideal pooping form. Our foresisters—who had their share of struggles but lucked out of having to always make sure the toilet seat was down—used to handle their ones and twos in a squatting position over the ground. Not only were their glutes probably better for it, but also, squatting at a 45-degree angle changes the position of the rectum so it can let poop out with minimal effort.

PERIOD≋POURRI

BECAUSE
WOMEN
POOP,
TOO!

"Getting my period is a real delight!"
said no woman ever. On top of cramps,
bloating, fatigue, and intense cravings
for soft pretzels and lingering hugs,
women also poop more on their periods.
Scientists think it's because the hormones
that make your uterus contract, called
prostaglandins, can get into your bowels
and cause them to contract as well,
meaning more bowel movements during
that time of the month.

PERIODS ARE SHITTY

BOOKING IT
TO THE
BATHROOM

For some, being among the written word instinctively produces the urge to turd. In Japan it's called the "Mariko Aoki phenomenon," after the woman who in 1985 first described the feeling of having to poop upon entering a bookstore. There's no known medical cause for the condition, but it's theorized that it may stem from the smell of ink and paper, which reminds us of reading on the toilet at home. Backed up? Try adding a hearty dose of prose to your diet.

POOPING IN SPACE? IT'S IN THE BAG.

Gender bias is just as present in zero G as it is here on Earth. NASA launched its first astronaut into space in 1961 but waited more than two decades to send a woman (Sally Ride, in 1983). But according to astronaut and author Mary Robinette Kowal, women's ascent to the stars wasn't delayed due to technical difficulties on the toilet for women specifically, as some have suggested. Apparently, peeing and pooping in space is a problem for both sexes, but women have it a bit harder.

Male astronauts originally used condom-like apparatuses to relieve themselves in space, but these gadgets often failed and released pee into their suits or the shuttle cabin because—you guessed it—the astronauts had lied about the size of sheath they needed. A man lying about his condom size? Well, I never! *Dramatic gasp!*

Luckily, when NASA finally opted to send women into space, they created a peeing and pooping system that was less penis-specific and is now used by both sexes. It involves a funnel, a tube, suction, and a bag. But without gravity, poop doesn't "break off" as it would on a regular toilet, and one must reach back and "help" with special gloves. On the off chance that this suction system breaks, peeing and pooping becomes a little more, ahem, involved: both male and female astronauts use "manual" collection and must tape bags to their butts when it's time to "go."

HIS & HERS

HIS & HERS

HIS & HERS

HOW DID WE GET HERE?

If you've ever wondered why bathrooms are separated by gender, the answer lies in some archaic sexist thinking from the early 1900s called the "Separate Sphere Ideology." Essentially, this idiotic ideology suggested that men and women should stay in their gender lanes; a woman's lane being in the home and a man's lane being outside of it. Sure, a woman's place is in the house...the House of Representatives.

Of course, as women began to leave homemaking for money making, the structure of public spaces had to change, and gender-segregated restrooms became commonplace under the uniform building code "movement" in the 1920s.

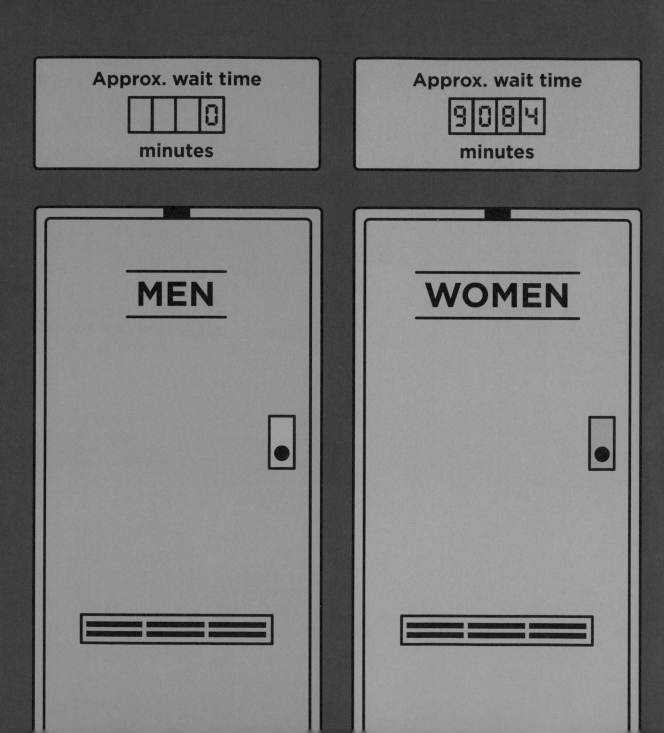

IT'S A MAN'S WORLD,
AND WE'RE JUST POOPIN' IN IT.

As a woman, have you ever been at an event and thought to yourself, "Wow, I really gotta go, but the women's restroom line is going to be approximately 459 miles long, so is it even worth trying? Do I think I can just hold it for the rest of this?" You know how many times a man has thought this in his lifetime? Uhhhhh...probably zero times. They're in, they're out, they've moved on with their lives. Whereas women spend so much time in restroom lines, we've all probably met one of our best friends in one, bonding over the shared trauma of hoping our bladders don't explode during the intermission of *Cats*.

Because most people who design public restrooms are men, it makes sense that women aren't exactly prioritized in their designs. In theory, it's easier to copy and paste the size and layout of a men's restroom to a women's—sans urinals, of course—but doing so disregards the needs, and frankly, the existence of women as a separate entity from men.

Just because the square footage of a restroom may be equal doesn't mean its capacity and utility are equal. Men have the luxury of urinals and speed, while women—who must deal with things like periods, rompers (yeah, we're talking having to get fully naked), changing babies, and wiping—not only need to take longer to use the restroom but also require more space to take care of business. Yet they're usually given the same amount of bathroom real estate as men.

WOMAN INVENTS PLUMBING, CRACKS PORCELAIN CEILING

Before the trailblazing ingenuity of a clever fourteenth-century Englishwoman named Alice Wade, your options for getting rid of poop were pretty limited: going in a bucket and chucking it out the window, pooping in a giant communal hole, or sneaking out to the woods and burying it. All not-so-pleasant options. Alice invented a wooden pipe system that ran underneath neighboring houses and dumped her ones and twos into a street. Sure, it had some kinks, like being a bit bothersome to people on said street or the aforementioned neighbors, who suffered the consequences when the pipe clogged, but hey, it was a solid start.

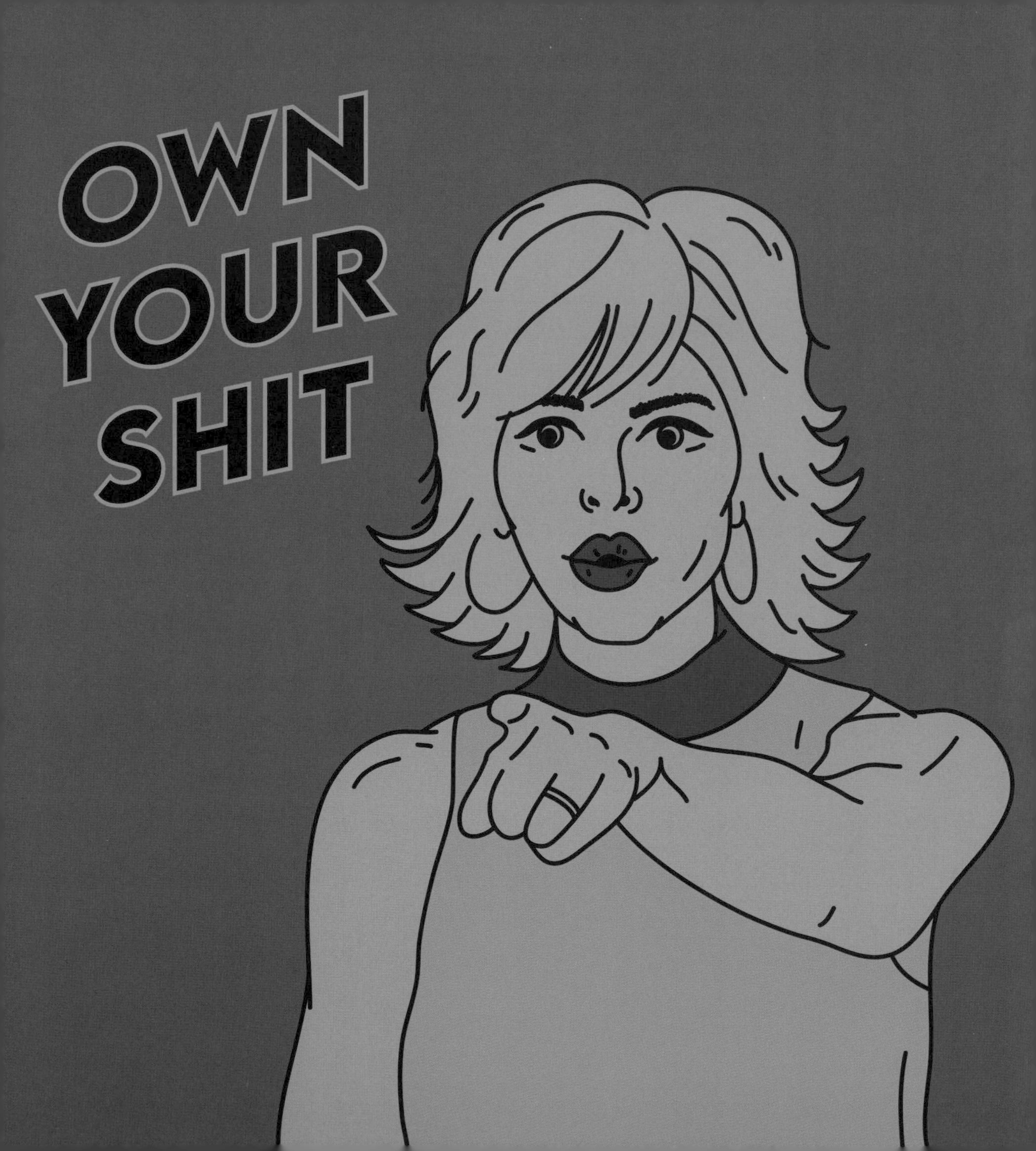
OWN
YOUR
SHIT

AND ALL THE SMELLS THAT COME WITH IT

It's amusing to imagine that when Lisa Rinna and her iconic lips uttered her infamous catchphrase, "Own your shit," for the first time as an official Real Housewife, she was intentionally rallying women around the idea of owning, well, their real shit. Then you could say she was inciting a movement—a bowel movement, if you will.

Imagine a world where poop doesn't stink. Now forget about it, because unless you're eating literal roses for breakfast, lunch, and dinner, that'll never happen. Turns out, science has proven that there are major differences in poop odors between men and women. That's because bacteria is one of the main components of poop (making up about one-third of its mass), and males and females have different blends of gut bacteria. And it's because of this that the types of gases produced may also vary between men and women, and, as we all know, some gases smell, well, less pleasant than others.

THE WOMEN OF CONGRESS WILL BE RECOGNIZED

Women have been figures (hidden and otherwise) in government for centuries, but the fact that they, too, had functioning digestive systems and needed the means to relieve themselves wasn't taken into account until … wait for it … 2011! Congressional women didn't have their own bathrooms on the House floor until 2011! Women in the Senate hadn't fared much better, getting their own in 1993. What the fart?!

As the #LadyGang of the Senate grew, more restrooms were needed to accommodate them, obviously, but they had to wait until 2013. 2013! And even though that was a win—albeit small and long overdue—for the women of Capitol Hill, it's definitely a quantity-over-quality situation. Apparently, these restrooms still lack things like period-stuff dispensers and baby-changing tables. Let's hope we Pelo-see some improvements for lady reps soon!

TODAY'S TOPIC

DO WOMEN *REALLY* NEED BATHROOMS?

THAT'S SOME (I)BS!

All in all, women have more gastrointestinal disorders, like irritable bowel syndrome (IBS), than men. IBS occurs two to six times more often in women than in men. Women with IBS have super-sensitivity to irritants—like gas—that wouldn't bother many people. It seems to be caused by the way nerves in the intestines send messages to the brain, and how the brain relays those messages to the gut. And surprise, surprise—emotional stress makes IBS worse.

WHEN IN ROME

Ancient Rome's public latrines (just a fancy old word for "toilet") were a total free-for-all (or should we say "poop-for-all"?). Men, women, and children all sat side by side and did their ones and twos at the same time.

Perhaps we could learn a thing or two from this page in history when it comes to restroom inclusivity and the benefits it affords people of all ages and genders. With a wee more privacy, of course.

OK, LADIES,
NOW LET'S GET IN
POOP-FORMATION

For our foremothers, pooping privacy wasn't always easy to come by. When pioneers were heading west in covered wagons back in the Gold Rush days, the men would simply find a shrub or pop a squat on the open range, while the women would form elaborate protective circles to shield one another. All of the women caravanning together would stand in a circle, facing out, holding their skirts out to the side to form a wall. Kind of like the beach towel changing room you build around your friends in an I-need-to-change-out-of-this-wet-bathing-suit pinch. And nothing says, "Nothing to see here!" like a perfect circle of women in the middle of the Oregon Trail. Then, one at a time, they'd take turns going to the bathroom in the middle of the circle. But these women truly had each other's backsides, and we stan that kind of girl power!

PEE-FORMANCE ANXIETY

Despite taking pride in their indecent deuces and flatulence, men actually have a hard time mustering the courage to urinate in front of other men, especially if they're in close proximity to each other. Quite simply, they're pee shy. And in one study, the authors monitored a row of three urinals and clocked an average of 4.9 seconds if the male subject was all alone, 6.2 seconds if there was a one-urinal buffer, and 8.4 seconds if there was someone at the neighboring urinal. Can someone turn on the faucet, please?

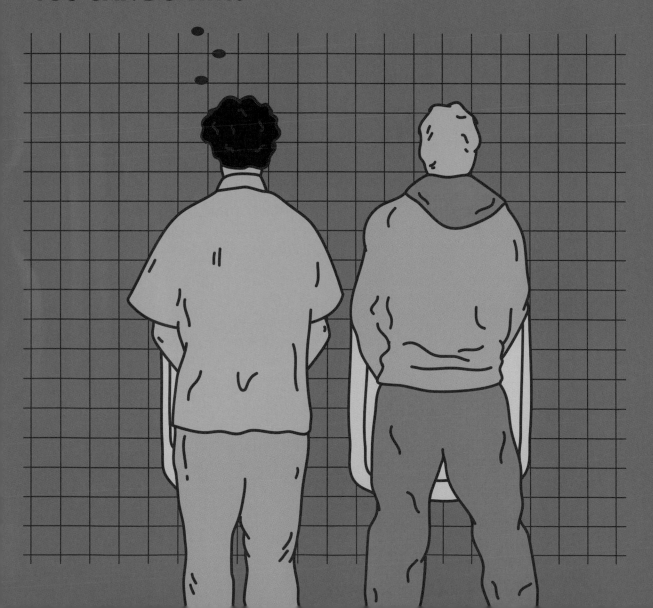

DOUBLE
THE
TROUBLE

One study that examined the amount of time each gender spends in public restrooms found that, on average, women spend twice as long as men do on the toilet. Generally, women outlasted men by a full minute (61.5 seconds).

It could be because we're scrolling our Instagram feeds (80% of men and 69% of women use their phone on the toilet), but it's more likely that we're doing all the fun little routine things men don't have to worry about, like removing our pants, skirts, entire jumpsuits, or whatever bottoms are the trend that season, every single time we have to one or two. Then we have to sit—or hover, depending on the ick factor—unroll toilet paper, maybe check for period blood or any other "situation" that might arise below (you really never know what you're going to find down there), redo whatever wardrobe contraption we've weaseled out of, and wash our hands. When you think about it, it's really a miracle that we only take an extra minute.

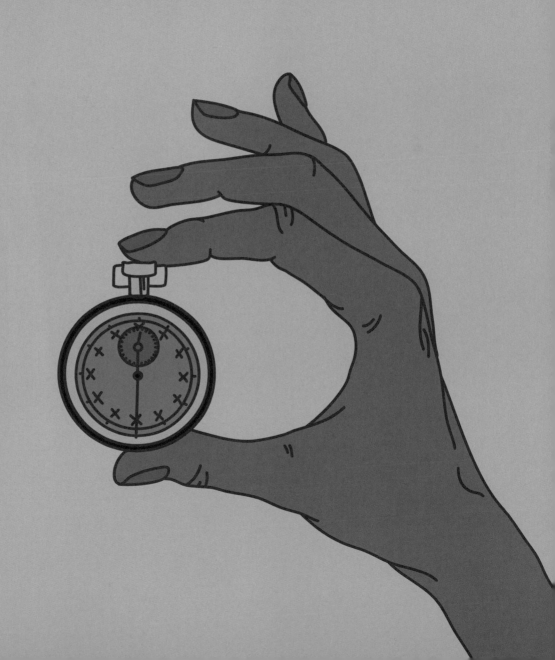

PROPER TOILET SQUAT FORM

DO:

ALLOW YOUR MIND TO WANDER AND PRETEND YOU ARE IN THE COMFORT OF YOUR OWN TOILET

DON'T:

LOOK TOO CLOSELY AT YOUR SURROUNDINGS AS YOU MIGHT GET DIZZY AND FAINT

DROP IT LIKE IT'S
HOT

AND COVERED IN PEE, PUBES, AND IDK, THE PLAGUE

Men may think we're spending all that time in chair pose or up in the gym working on our fitness to sculpt our butts to round, firm perfection, but they're wrong. We're really putting in all that booty werk to train our glutes for the inevitable and dreaded public-toilet "hover." To the gentleman reader: it should be pretty self-explanatory, but if it's not, politely ask a woman to demonstrate "the hover." She knows, for she has lived through this traumatic ritual more times than she can count.

Only 2% of women sit directly on a public toilet seat (ladies, you are brave, and we salute you), but 85% of women usually hover over the toilet, and 12% put down paper before sitting. You know, like when the seat covers are out—and they usually are—so you gingerly create a cute little TP nest on the seat.

YOU DON'T WANNA KNOW
WHERE THOSE HANDS HAVE BEEN

It turns out that everyone lies about how much they wash their hands, but when it comes to who's lathering up after a twosie, there's a huge discrepancy between the genders. Women tend to wash their hands 69% of the time after peeing and 84% of the time after poopin' (remember, we do that; it's the title of the book), whereas men wash up 43% of the time after a wee and 78% of the time after "pinching one off."

C'mon guys, scrub-a-dub-dub! Better yet, let's make it hundreds across the board, because—gross.*

*Parts of this book were written during the COVID-19 pandemic, so if poop-covered hands weren't enough incentive to wash up, hopefully preventing the spread of a deadly virus has provided people with some extra motivation to reach for the soap.

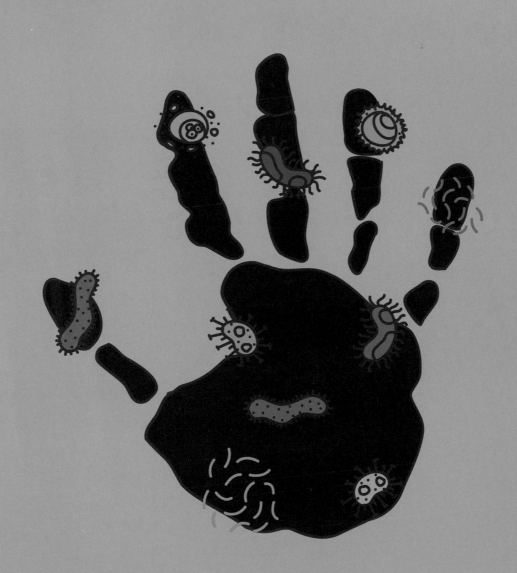

WHO CHOOSES WHICH STALL?

ACCORDING TO A SURVEY* OF BATHROOMGOERS' HABITS,

IF PRESENTED WITH THREE EMPTY STALLS, MEN:

- Go left 28% of the time
- Go straight ahead 40% of the time
- Go to the right 32% of the time

PRESENTED WITH THAT SAME TRIO, WOMEN:

- Go left 34% of the time
- Go straight ahead 29% of the time
- Go to the right 37% of the time

BUT WHEN THE LEFT STALL IS OCCUPIED, MEN:

- Head to the far right 73% of the time

WOMEN, UNDER THE SAME CIRCUMSTANCE:

- Head to the far right 65% of the time

* from *The First Really Important Survey of American Habits*
by Mel Poretz and Barry Sinrod

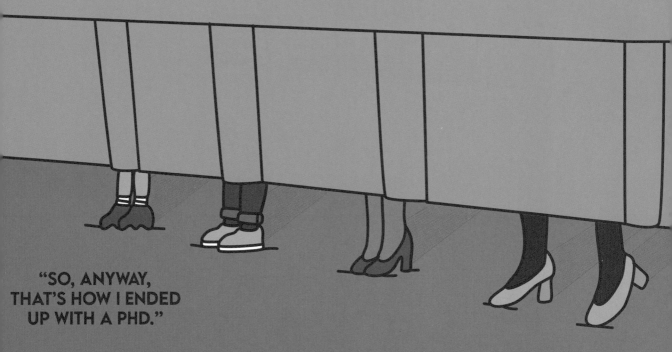

LET'S HAVE A PEE-PEE.

LOCK THE DOORS TIGHT.

It's probably pretty clear by now that the differences between how men and women conduct themselves in restrooms are numerous and vast. But one of the biggest differences is the way we treat each other, members of the same gender, in our respective relief areas.

For men, once the restroom door swings shut, they go from amigos to a-me-go-incognito. Even the best of buds only pay each other civil inattention—just briefly acknowledging the other person is there and then pretending they're not—in the general restroom, but running into the same friend at the adjoining urinal dictates nonperson treatment, like fully pretending they're not even there to begin with or acting like they're just another object.

While the same can be true for women—it's not always easy to make new friends when nature is really calling—many times we find the restroom to be a place of bonding and sharing. Think about it: sometimes we even intentionally go there together, linked arm in arm. Sometimes we go as far as to use it as a confessional of sorts. Trust me, many of my deepest, darkest secrets have been revealed behind a stall door. And that is where I hope they'll stay.

DUDE
OR
DOG?

You know how dogs go around peeing on everything to mark their territory? Well, it turns out, men do the same thing to urinals. And if you're thinking, "Duh, they pee on them, that's what urinals are for," well, I have news for you. They're not just peeing on them.

Of all the things men could do before using a urinal, those with a more territorial streak like to spit in them. Yes, spit. "It's a way to appear stronger and mark your space," says Boise State sociologist Robert McCarl. "Males are more concerned about turf than women are. You get a group of males together, and there is a lot of posturing going on." So, yeah, there's a gross fact about men and urinals you probably didn't know, or want to know, before.

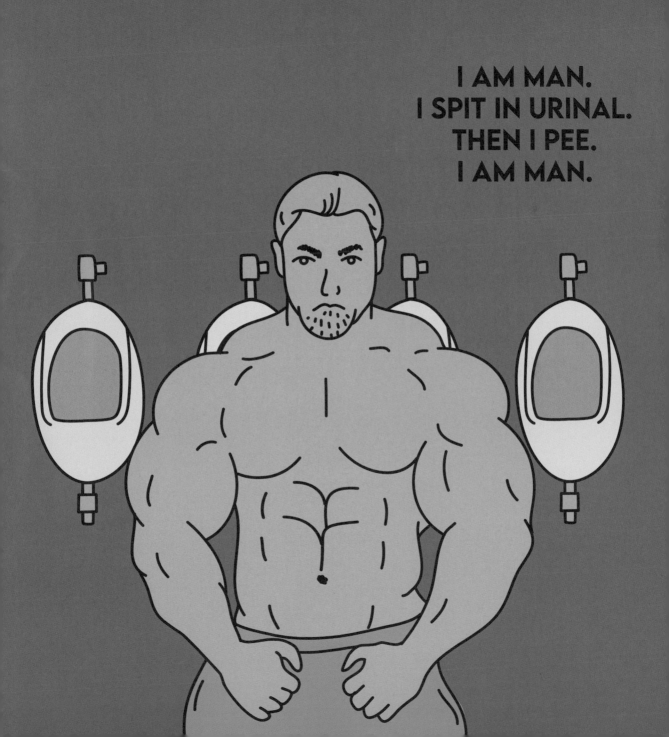

69% **OF MEN** DON'T WASH THEIR HANDS

69% **OF MEN** DON'T WASH THEIR HANDS

69% **OF MEN** DON'T WASH THEIR HANDS

69% **OF MEN** DON'T WASH THEIR HANDS

69% **OF MEN** DON'T WASH THEIR HANDS

69% **OF MEN** DON'T WASH THEIR HANDS

69% **OF MEN** DON'T WASH THEIR HANDS

69% **OF MEN** DON'T WASH THEIR HANDS

69% **OF MEN** DON'T WASH THEIR HANDS

69% **OF MEN** DON'T WASH THEIR HANDS

69% **OF MEN** DON'T WASH THEIR HANDS

69% **OF MEN** DON'T WASH THEIR HANDS

69% **OF MEN** DON'T WASH THEIR HANDS*

*According to a study cited by the Centers for Disease Control and Prevention.

SIGNS SEND MIXED SIGNALS, *APPARENTLY*

For reasons beyond comprehension and, well, logic, signs reminding people to wash their hands work for women, but not for men. Maybe it's because men don't like being told what to do by inanimate objects? According to one study, the percentage of women who washed their hands increased from 61% to 97% as a result of signage, while signs led to *less* compliance from men, dropping from 37% to 35%. C'mon guys, is it really so hard to follow directions?

Male or female, young or old, everyone lies about hand-washing. For shame, people. For shame.

Men and women alike lie about how much they wash their hands. Only 56% of us even bother claiming to wash every time. Another study discovered that only 32% of food-handlers wash their hands, even though it's required. Gross. Now, if you'll excuse me, I need to go wash my own mouth out with soap.

EVERYONE IS A DIRTY LIAR.

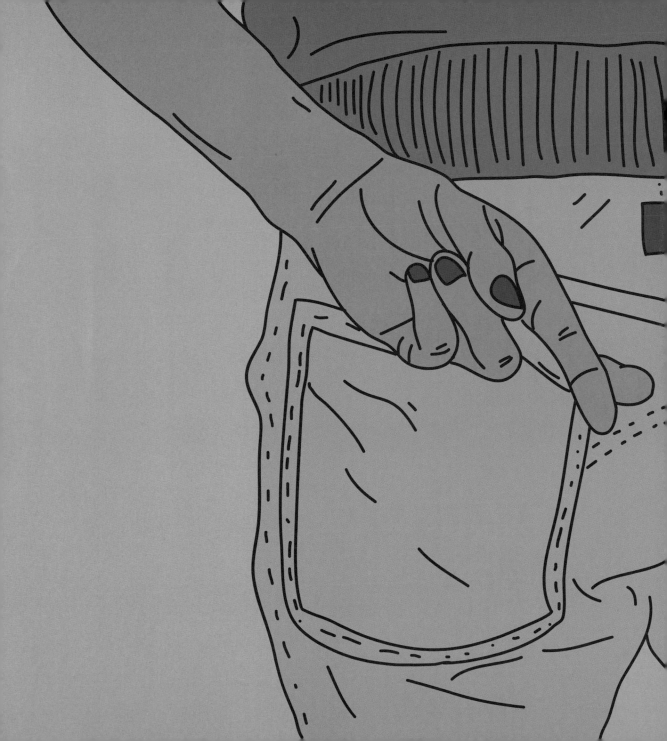

888-6969
Text me
Be my baby
LOL POOP
chicks rule
HOTTIE
HIT ME UP
poop here
LOVE YOU
farts r kool
NICE BUTT
you're hot
love you mean it
YOU + ME = A GOOD TIME
hugs not drugs
FOR A GOOD TIME CALL 541·2601
yo momma so fine

FOR A GOOD TIME,
CALL

Who among us hasn't indulged in the guilty pleasure of some graffiti while in a bar bathroom? Especially a real divey one. But have you ever wondered how our graffiti styles differ between genders?

The renowned sexologist Alfred Kinsey found that 86% of graffiti in men's bathrooms was erotic in nature, compared to just 25% in women's restrooms. But guess what? The majority of what's written on the walls of a men's room is 75% homosexual in nature. Also, men compose graffiti that's more likely to proposition readers, more likely to be a freehand doodle, and more likely to contain the artist's initials.

Women, on the other hand, draw graffiti that's more romantic, more interactive, but also way more likely to insult rivals. And when they do write insulting graffiti, they focus on physical appearance and cheating. So, basically, the walls of a women's room are just one big burn book.

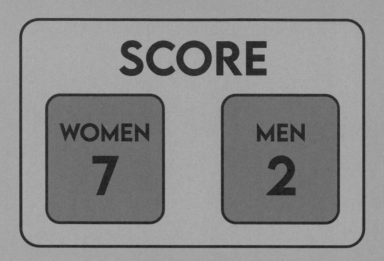

You've heard of the gender wage gap, but have you ever heard of the TP-usage gap? It's a thing. If toilet paper usage were a competition, women would come out ahead every time. Women use way more toilet paper than men, which isn't exactly a huge surprise. We do have to use it EVERY TIME, while a simple jiggle works for men half of the time. So, what's the big difference? Women use an average of seven toilet-paper squares per visit, and men use only two.

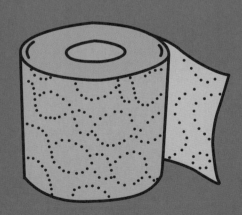
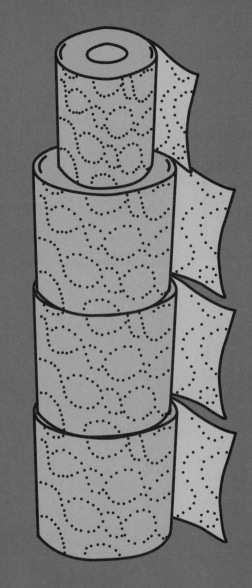

MEN   **WOMEN**

OPPOSITES

ATTRACT

ATTRACT

OPPOSITES

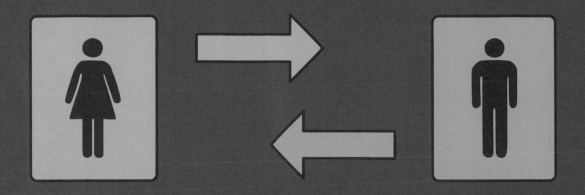

Have you ever gotten fed up with the women's restroom line, looked longingly at the empty men's room, and just said, "Eff it! I'm going in!" Turns out, we're more likely to have the balls to do it when we're less likely to see balls if we do it—that is, if it's a single-stall, lockable-door scenario. Also, women are significantly more likely to use the men's room than men are to use the women's room.

And it seems like that's kind of okay with both sides. Both men and women tend to agree that it's more acceptable for women to use the men's room than for men to use the women's room.

~~WOMEN'S~~

~~MEN'S~~

HUMANS' ROOM

Whatever you call them—unisex, gender-inclusive, gender-neutral, mixed-sex, all-gender, or just toilets—inclusive restrooms can help us solve a lot of the problems created by gender separation.

How, you ask? Well, first, they're beneficial for people with disabilities, the elderly, and anyone who needs the help of someone of another gender or sex. They're also valuable for parents wishing to accompany young children who haven't quite gotten the hang of potty training or have concerns about safety.

Transgender and nonbinary people also benefit greatly from inclusive restrooms. Even where their right to use gendered bathrooms is legally protected, they still might not feel comfortable or safe in one. According to a 2009 survey, 68% of transgender survey respondents were "denied access to, verbally harassed in, and/or physically assaulted in public bathrooms."

It's also cheaper to construct a single gender-neutral bathroom than two smaller segregated facilities. So, really, it's a win-win-win for every body. Need we say more?

RESTROOM

THIS RESTROOM MAY BE USED BY
ANY PERSON, REGARDLESS OF
GENDER IDENTITY OR EXPRESSION

FIGHTING FOR THE RIGHT TO POTTY

Believe it or not—no, actually, believe it, because it's real and it's important—there are actual laws prohibiting people from using the restroom that matches their gender or nonbinary identity. "Bathroom bills" are laws that limit access to public toilets by gender, and that specifically target transgender people.

It's not up for debate as to whether or not these bills that exclude transgender individuals from restrooms are a violation of human rights. No matter your gender identity, you're a human.

The facts are, these so-called bathroom bills don't make public restrooms any safer for cisgender people, and actually, they make public restrooms less safe for both transgender people and gender-nonconforming people. There have been no cases of a transgender person attacking a cisgender person in a public restroom. By contrast, many transgender people have been verbally, physically, and sexually harassed or attacked by cisgender people in public restrooms.

There's a reason many people call pooping "doing your business": it is indeed your own business and no one else's.

Well, reader, you did it. You opened this book—probably on a toilet—and you learned a whole shitload about pooping and how this normal thing we all do is pretty sexist, especially for women.

So, what now?

I don't know, exactly. Maybe you go about your day feeling a little lighter in the gut, but a little heftier in knowledge. Or maybe you feel empowered by the awareness that women, all women, poop. Even the most powerful, feminist icons among us. Oprah? Poops. Beyoncé? Poops. Elizabeth Warren? Poops. Cher? Poops. Ruth Bader Ginsburg? She poops, and it's supreme AF.

Now, go forth and poop. Poop like no one's smelling! Poop like the feminist utopia of tax-exempt tampons, unisex restrooms, and perpetually down toilet seats depends on it!

Because women poop. And that's the truth.

SPOILER ALERT:

WOMEN POOP!

ABOUT THE CONTRIBUTORS

Bonnie Miller is just a gal who likes words, poopin', and smashing the patriarchy.

Nicole Narváez is a visual artist from Brooklyn, New York, and an associate creative director at a NY advertising agency. Nicole runs an art business and Instagram page (@Narvaez_Art), where she creates feminist, political, and societal artwork. She also oil paints and likes to rock climb, though not usually at the same time. To check out Nicole's less poop-related work, visit narvaezart.co.